330.9704
R21m

94505

DATE DUE

WITHDRAWN

The Myth of the Appalachian Brain Drain

A Case Study of West Virginia

by

RICHARD D. RAYMOND

West Virginia University Library
Morgantown
1972

Copyright © 1972
West Virginia University Foundation
Morgantown, West Virginia
Standard Book Number 87012-120-0
Library of Congress Catalog Card Number 72-187762
All Rights Reserved
Printed by McClain Printing Company
Parsons, West Virginia

The publication of this book was
made possible by a grant from the
WEST VIRGINIA UNIVERSITY
FOUNDATION

Acknowledgements

The successful completion of this study would have been impossible without the cooperation of a number of individuals. The study was actually conceived by Professor William H. Miernyk who provided invaluable assistance in devising and circulating the questionnaire and in editing and interpreting the final results. The registrars of the seventeen West Virginia colleges and universities were very cooperative in supplying the names and addresses of their graduating seniors. Data processing was capably handled by Guy Johnson and Ronald McCormick. Mrs. Barbara Fisher supplied many helpful editorial suggestions on the final draft. I also benefitted greatly from numerous discussions with colleagues and students at both West Virginia University and Kent State University. Needless to say, I alone am responsible for the opinions expressed in the study.

Table of Contents

Foreword by William H. Miernyk ix
Chapter 1—The Economic Effects of a Brain Drain .. 1
Chapter 2—Survey Results 15
Chapter 3—The Role of Public Policy 43
    Tables 55
    Appendix A 71
    Appendix B 75

Foreword

The depressed condition of the Appalachian economy has been so widely discussed that by now it has become legendary. The causes of this depression are also generally well known: the precipitous decline of employment in the bituminous coal fields—particularly after the famed "mechanization agreement" of 1950 between the UMW and the coal operators—the steady erosion of agricultural employment, and the failure of alternative job opportunities to develop in Appalachian urban centers.

But Appalachia is surrounded by metropolitan areas and, along with the rest of the nation's metropolitan centers, they grew substantially during the 1950s and 1960s. Reaction to the combination of declining job opportunities in Appalachia and the growth of new jobs in cities surrounding the region was predictable. There has been an exodus of Appalachian residents, although net out-migration dropped from 2.2 million persons in the 1950s to 1.4 million during the 1960s.

Economists, particularly those who are persuaded that the best decisions are those made by impersonal market forces, tend to regard this as a healthy adjustment to economic change. This is the type of adjustment that is predicted by neo-classical economic theory, a branch of applied logic that has enjoyed an unexpected revival in recent years. Interregional flows of labor and capital are necessary, according to this way of thinking, if the economy is to adapt to disturbances engendered by technological change, changing consumer preferences, and other dynamic influences on the economy. "Labor" and "capital" when treated in this way are regarded as homogeneous units.

Labor economists, and others who have studied the phenomenon of migration, have found that the characteristics of migrants are not those of a random sample of the population. In general, those who migrate from depressed areas are relatively young, relatively well educated and without family, property, or other encumbrances that might hinder their movement to another part of the country. Migration, therefore, is a selective process, and if this process continues for a substantial length of time it can alter the characteristics of the population left behind.

The process of selective migration is not, of course, limited to depressed areas. A region (or a country) need not experience actual economic distress before it begins to lose some of its younger and better educated residents. This can happen any time that there are substantial differences in the *relative* returns to educated workers among regions or among nations. The migration of educated workers—which has come to be called a "brain drain"—has been studied with some degree of intensity in recent years. The monograph which Dr. Raymond has written is an important contribution to the growing literature on the brain drain.

Foreword

The study which is reported in the following pages is based on original data which Dr. Raymond collected by means of a survey. The survey was limited to institutions of higher education in West Virginia, and Dr. Raymond is careful not to imply that his findings extend beyond the area that he studied. But in many ways West Virginia is representative of all of the parts of Appalachia that have experienced economic distress. It is the only state that lies entirely within the Appalachian region, and it is the only state that has the dubious distinction of a steadily declining population since 1950. It is a predominantly rural state although there is little agriculture in West Virginia. A number of medium sized urban areas are found in West Virginia and some of these have prospered in recent years. But adaptation to structural change has been slow in the Mountain State, and many young West Virginians have left the state in search of better economic opportunities elsewhere.

The out-migration of a substantial number of young college graduates has provided an interesting and perhaps unique opportunity to study the phenomenon of a regional "brain drain." It is important to point out that Dr. Raymond did not attempt to estimate the *net* results of migration out of and into West Virginia. He has focused his attention on the characteristics of out-migrants, and of their contemporaries who elected to remain in West Virginia after completing their education in the state. He also has developed a conceptual framework which places the important issues involved in a discussion of human migration in proper perspective.

The findings of Dr. Raymond's study may come as a surprise to some readers. They should also encourage the planners and policy makers at all levels of government who are devoting their time, energy and part of the nation's resources to the goal of regional growth and development.

William H. Miernyk
Director, Regional
Research Institute

Chapter 1

The Economic Effects of a Brain Drain

Changes in Local Income

In an area experiencing a "brain drain," there tends to be a reduction in both aggregate and per capita income. This is what one would expect, since the educated individuals moving out of the area have incomes, or income potential, above the average for all of the area's residents. A nation's security and even its existence may be threatened by reduction in aggregate wealth which involves a loss of economic and military power.[1] But this consideration would not apply to a state or regional brain drain. In the latter case, it is the welfare of individuals that is of primary importance. Thus the use of statistics that relate to geographic areas rather than to groups of individuals may lead to mis-

---

[1] For opposing views on the validity of this argument see Herbert B. Grubel and Anthony D. Scott, "The International Flow of Human Capital," *American Economic Review*, Vol. LVI, No. 2 (May 1966), p. 269; and Constantine Michalopoulos, "Labor Migration and Optimum Population," *Kylos*, Vol. 21 (1968), pp. 137-38.

leading conclusions. A reduction in aggregate income does not necessarily imply a reduction in the income of the individuals remaining in the area. Since this study deals with factors capable of affecting the welfare of the persons who remain in the area, aggregate data are not particularly relevant or useful.[2]

The Cost of Education and the Brain Drain

The demise of a widely held view can be a very slow and painful process particularly when that view has a reasonable "ring" to it, but "the difficulty lies, not in the new ideas, but in escaping from the old ones..."[3] For example, some contend that educational costs are lost to the source area and gained by the destination area when individuals migrate, involving a simple transfer of human capital. The source area creates this capital by financing an individual's education and then loses it when migration occurs. This view has been criticized on a number of occasions.[4] Yet it seems to persist in

[2] The situation of the migrants themselves is, of course, also important; but when migration is voluntary it may safely be assumed that the migrant's position has been improved. See Grubel and Scott, *op. cit.*, p. 270, and Burton A. Weisbrod, "Discussion," *American Economic Review*, Vol. LVI, No. 2 (May 1966), p. 278.

[3] John Maynard Keynes, *The General Theory of Employment Interest and Money* (Macmillan and Company, 1936), Preface p. viii.

[4] Burton A. Weisbrod, *External Benefits of Public Education: An Economic Analysis* (Industrial Relations Section, Princeton University, 1964), Chapter 4, and Grubel and Scott, *op. cit.*

The Economic Effects of a Brain Drain 3

varying degrees, both in academic and nonacademic circles.[5]

Consider a specified number of individuals publicly educated in area A. If they migrate from area A to area B, in what sense can we say that A has lost and B has gained the cost of their education? First assume that these individuals are always paid the full value of the extra output they produce as a result of their education (their marginal products). In general, this will hold true if the presence of these individuals does not affect the output of other members of the work force. The existence of something which affects the output of others is termed an externality. For instance, an educated individual generates a *positive externality* when his presence raises the productivity of the remainder of the work force. In addition, assume that each individual always pays in taxes precisely the extra (marginal) cost of the public services he consumes. An excess of taxes paid

---

[5] Recent statements by academicians tend to be qualified and guarded, but the policy suggestions made by Johnson and Boulding for instance, imply that they regard the cost of education as at least a close approximation to the costs inflicted upon the source area by the migrant. See H. G. Johnson, "An 'Internationalist' Model," and K. E. Boulding, "The 'National' Importance of Human Capital," both in Walter Adams, editor, *The Brain Drain* (Macmillan and Company, 1968). For repeated references to the importance of this concept to policy makers in the U.S. see Niles M. Hansen, *Rural Poverty and the Urban Crisis* (Indiana University Press, 1970).

over the marginal cost of public services consumed may be termed *excess* taxation.[6]

If these assumptions are valid, it is obvious that area A does "lose" the cost of educating these individuals. The remaining residents of A have paid for this education and they receive nothing in return. But it is equally obvious that area B does not gain this amount or, for that matter, anything at all. The migrants contribute in taxes only what they receive in public services, and they do not enhance the well-being of the residents of B by generating external effects. The gain corresponding to (but not necessarily equal to) the loss suffered by area A is realized completely by the individuals who received the free public education in A. Furthermore, the educated individuals would receive, and the remaining residents of A would lose, the cost of this education regardless of where the educated individuals chose to live and work.

Thus, the cost of education *per se* is obviously not lost because of migration. The true costs associated with migration may, in specific cases, be approximately equal to the cost of educating the migrants, but there is no *a priori* reason for expecting this to be so. It is essentially an empirical question that depends upon the degree to which our assumptions are valid.

Now suppose that the amount of excess taxation is

[6] These assumptions do not exhaust the gains and losses associated with migration. They are, however, among the most important, and exhaustive treatment would serve only to complicate the exposition without altering any of the conclusions.

positively related to income, and positive externalities are associated with the employment of educated individuals. The excess taxation and the positive externalities that would have been present in A will now measure the true cost of migration to the remaining residents of A. Furthermore, this amount will measure the true cost of migration to A's residents regardless of where the impact of educational financing falls: upon A's residents, the individuals themselves, or a federal government encompassing both areas. The true cost of migration must be an amount which can be avoided by prohibiting migration, or an amount which will be lost if and only if migration occurs. It follows that the true cost of migration is completely independent of the method of financing the individual's education even if the true cost of migration happens by chance to be precisely equal to the cost of education.[7] Thus, it may be concluded that a number of frequently advanced solutions to the brain drain problem are wide of the mark.

Both Boulding and Johnson suggest solving the brain drain problem by financing education through student loans.[8] This, Boulding argues, would mean that "a per-

[7] The cost to area A is, of course, not necessarily equal to the gain in area B. The gain in B is given by the sum of the excess taxation and positive externalities generated in B by the migration.
[8] Boulding, *op. cit.*, pp. 114-16, and Johnson, *op. cit.*, p. 87. Both authors are concerned primarily with the international brain drain, but their analysis also may be applied to the interregional case.

son who migrated to a richer country in the hope of increasing his income would still have to pay back the cost of his education with interest to the country of his origin which is thereby compensated for his loss."[9] The most obvious deficiency with this solution is that the cost of an individual's education may differ widely, *in either direction,* from the true costs imposed upon his country of origin by his migration.[10]

There is, however, an additional and perhaps more serious objection to this solution. Since every student would have to repay the cost of his education regardless of where he chose to live, a country would gain no extra payment from the individual who left the country. That is to say, the payment made by the individual would not be contingent upon his decision to migrate.[11] Yet his migration would continue to carry with it all the losses associated with excess taxation and externalities. It is true that by transferring a major item from the public to the private sector the student loan plan would ease the

[9] Boulding, *op. cit.*, p. 115.

[10] Johnson suggests that one reason for concentrating on the cost of education is the great difficulty involved in measuring the other losses, *op. cit.*, p. 88.

[11] This objection may be eliminated by requiring the repayment of education costs only by those who migrate. But the difficulty resulting from the inequality between the actual cost of migration and the cost of education would remain. In addition, this procedure would result in an inefficient restriction of migration from a global point of view since the decision making process would not take into account the gains accruing to the destination areas.

state's fiscal requirements, thus making it easier for the state to bear the cost of a brain drain. But the same effect would result from the extension of the benefit principle of taxation into other areas which are equally unrelated to the migration problem.

Whether an individual should, in general, be required to repay the cost of his education is a separate and important question. As presently constituted, our system rejects a direct application of the benefit principle of taxation to education. The progressive income tax, given the strong positive relationship between income and education, can be interpreted as an indirect application of this principle to education. In the future, the public may choose to ask that an individual bear the cost of his own education beyond some specified minimal level. But the decision of individuals to stay or to leave the state in which they were educated seems to be a totally irrelevant consideration.

In summary, it is impossible to conclude that the cost of educating an individual generally represents an accurate measure of the economic losses generated by his migration. Only pragmatism can justify requiring migrants to repay the costs of their education; this may be the only practical method of recovering anything from the migrant.[12]

---

[12] For further views on the cost of education issue, see Harry G. Johnson, "The Economics of the 'Brain Drain': The Canadian Case," *Minerva*, Vol. 3, No. 3 (Spring 1965), pp. 302-3; Grubel and Scott, *op. cit.*, p. 272; and Harry G. Johnson's "Discussion," p. 283; Enrique Oteiza, "Emigration of Engineers from Argen-

Actual Economic Costs of Migration

The magnitude of the economic losses resulting from migration is extremely difficult to estimate. Most discussions of these losses tend to center around the international case. But there appear to be important differences, at least in terms of magnitude, when the interregional case is considered. The major costs may be separated conveniently into private sector and public sector costs.

Private Sector Costs: If the value of services performed by the migrant for the residents of the area is exactly equal to the money value paid by the residents for these services, then clearly the two will precisely offset one another. This would leave the residents' wellbeing unchanged. If, however, the value of the services exceeds the money value paid for them, then the residents in the area the migrant leaves will suffer a loss.

Externalities: Externalities associated with both production and consumption may give services provided by the migrant a greater value than the price paid for them in the marketplace. Consumption externalities occur when individuals other than the buyer of the service are benefited. Since the seller is unable to charge for these extra benefits, their value will represent a net loss to the residents of the area when he leaves. Perhaps the best

tina: A Case of Latin American 'Brain Drain'," *International Labor Review* (1965), pp. 445-61; and Burton A. Weisbrod, *External Benefits of Public Education* (Industrial Relations Section, Princeton University, 1964), pp. 41-42.

example of consumption externalities occurs in the provision of medical services. When an individual purchases medical services for his own benefit, he often simultaneously reduces the probability that other members of the community will contract communicable diseases. There is no way in which a doctor may charge for the benefits received by the remainder of the community; thus, these extra benefits will be lost to the community with no compensating gain if the doctor migrates.

Production externalities present at the international level have been conveniently summarized by Harry Johnson:

> First, individuals . . . might have made scientific discoveries, or introduced improved methods of production or management that would have substantially increased the productivity of resources . . .
> Second, the members of a particular profession may generate externalities . . . by providing informal education . . . to their fellow citizens . . .
> Third, the emigration of professional people may involve a significant proportional reduction in their numbers . . . thereby perhaps lowering the income (marginal products) of cooperating factors of production . . .
> Fourth, the emigration of professional people, by reducing their absolute numbers . . . (may result in) diseconomies of scale of production. . . .[13]

Information dissemination across regional boundaries is undoubtedly free enough to render the first exter-

[13] Johnson, *op. cit.*, pp. 81-82.

nality insignificant. In addition, the third and fourth will prove important only if the emigration results in an economic scarcity in the affected occupations. If, however, migration occurs primarily because there is a lack of local demand for the individuals in question, then these externalities will not be present.[14]

Economic Rent: The same form of discrepancy will occur if educated individuals fail to appropriate all economic rent associated with the services they provide. In the present context, economic rent is simply the full value of his present services minus the value of his services in his next best alternative occupation. An individual usually will not agree to work for less than he could earn elsewhere, but he may be unable to command the full value of his services. The existence of perfect competition among buyers of these services would ensure the seller's receiving all of the rent; however, markets seldom are perfect enough to produce this result. Monopsony elements, combined with a lack of sellers' information, may generate significant rents which do not in fact accrue to the seller. Migration of the seller will result in the loss of these rents to the individuals who were appropriating them.

Consumer's Surplus: Finally, the monetary value

---

[14] For a discussion of this point in relation to international migration see Suffiah Kannappan, "The Brain Drain and Developing Countries," *International Labor Review*, Vol. 98, No. 1 (July 1968), pp. 1-26, and Don Patinkin, "A Nationalist Model," in Walter Adams, *op. cit.*, pp. 92-108. Specific references to the U.S. are contained in Hansen, *op. cit.*

placed on services sold directly to the consumer does not include the consumer's surplus generated by the service. Consumer's surplus refers to the difference between the amount actually paid for a service and the maximum amount the consumer would be willing to pay rather than to go without the service. Many services are clearly worth more to us than we are forced to pay for them; consumer's surplus is a measure of the difference involved. A reduction in the supply of the service will result in a lower level of consumer's surplus, but in this instance, an offsetting gain is present. The remaining suppliers of the service will experience an increase in producer's surplus brought about by the resulting higher price. Producer's surplus is the excess of the amount paid to the supplier of a service over the minimum a supplier would be willing to accept. The net loss is likely to be quite small, but the resulting redistribution of income may be significant.

Public Sector Costs: In the case of interregional migration, losses associated with excess taxation refer solely to state and local tax and expenditure structures. This would seem to reduce the importance of this factor considerably. The most progressive elements in the tax structure facing individuals are administered on a national scale. Sales and property taxes provide the bulk of local revenue, particularly in underdeveloped sections of the country. There is also some tendency to handle redistributive expenditures at the national level.

Grubel and Scott pointed out that both private and public losses may be a matter of temporary concern only.[15] If an identical replacement can be found for the migrant, this replacement will prevent further losses. If, however, the rents and externalities are peculiar to the migrant himself, then filling the vacant position with a replacement will not restore the entire lost value.

While it is difficult, if not impossible, to measure these losses, they are not necessarily insignificant. These losses may actually linger for a considerable period of time, while conditions stimulating migration may make it difficult to find a replacement.[16] Also, consumption externalities and perhaps consumer's surplus may prove to be highly significant. This is illustrated by the tremendous concern often exhibited over the loss of "the" doctor in isolated areas. On the other hand, it does seem that larger losses from these sources will be associated with a small number of specialized occupations rather than with the general out-migration of educated individuals.

Nonpecuniary Considerations

An economist accustomed to dealing with pecuniary factors might be tempted to end the argument here. But this would be erroneous since individuals may have importance which cannot be measured monetarily. A "brain drain" may be resisted simply because residents feel that it creates a poor image for their state. An individual may gain satisfaction from his state's ability to attract and retain educated personnel and generate a

---

[15] Grubel and Scott, *op. cit.*, p. 271.
[16] See Patinkin, *op. cit.*, p. 103.

high per capita income, even if this does not affect him economically.[17] There is an offsetting psychological factor represented by the pride taken in the accomplishment of ex-natives residing outside of the state.[18] However, there is little doubt that out-migration in general, and a "brain drain" in particular, are regarded as bad *per se* by residents of the affected regions. Continuing publicity emphasizing the negative aspects of out-migration serves to reinforce this opinion until, in many instances, it seems to be the primary determinant of public policy in the area.

This discussion of the losses generated by a brain drain gave little indication of the quantitative importance of the various factors considered. This will be remedied in part by presenting the questionnaire results.

[17] For a description of the attitudes of Kentuckians on the migration issue see Mary Jean Bowman and W. Warren Haynes, *Resources and People in East Kentucky* (The Johns Hopkins Press, 1963), pp. 251-54.

[18] The migrants may, of course, send back more than the publicity surrounding their activities. Direct monetary remittances are often made and a widespread group of articulate ex-natives may serve to acquaint the rest of the nation with both the problems and the attractions of a state or a region.

Chapter 2

Survey Results

Introduction

The information concerning location decisions presented in this chapter was gathered from questionnaires sent to 6,245 graduating seniors attending 17 West Virginia colleges and universities in the spring of 1969. The questionnaire and accompanying cover letter are reproduced in Appendix A. Responses came from 2,158 individuals which represented 34.6 percent of the total. The response rate varied from 22.5 to 53.9 percent among the various schools (see Appendix A Exhibit 3).

One must remember, however, in a study of this kind, that since the information deals only with individuals leaving the state, a false impression may be created concerning the size of the net outflow of college graduates. Data were not available for an accurate estimate of the number of college trained individuals moving into West Virginia, but the staff directory of West Virginia University contains information indicating that a substantial immigration of such individuals does occur. This can be seen in the percentage of West Virginia University employees receiving their degrees outside West Virginia:

Ph.D., 88; M.A., 47; and B.A., 27. There were also 181 persons on the W.V.U. staff who had earned their B.A.'s in West Virginia, left the state, and returned with either M.A.'s or Ph.D.'s. This form of re-migration is important and cannot be ignored in an evaluation of the migration "problem" confronting the state.

The Entire Sample

Table 1 summarizes much of the basic information gained from the entire sample.[1] Figures given in the first three sections are largely self-explanatory. The major points to be noted are that approximately 42 percent of the sample had accepted employment or planned to seek employment within the state of West Virginia and that, on the average, annual salaries in West Virginia were $850 below salaries paid in other areas.

Differences in Ability: It is often concluded that exceptional individuals are more likely to leave an underdeveloped area than are average individuals. A number of appealing intuitive arguments can be advanced in support of this conclusion. Employers will ordinarily prefer exceptional to average individuals, and, in the case of underdeveloped areas, higher salaries are paid away from home. Employers in other areas, therefore, should succeed in attracting a relatively larger portion of the state's exceptional individuals. It is further argued that

---

[1] All tables referred to in the text are given at the end of Chapter 3, preceding Appendix A. Data relating to the population parameters were unavailable thus making it impossible to test the results for response biases.

apart from monetary gains the exceptional individual benefits more by migrating than does the average individual. Access to expensive physical facilities and opportunities to exchange views with competent colleagues may be more important to the exceptional individual. Finally, preference differences among individuals also could account for the existence of a brain drain. If a greater proportion of exceptional individuals place a high value on amenities which are available only in developed areas, then, given the higher monetary awards available in developed areas, a brain drain obviously will occur.

The survey results, however, completely fail to demonstrate migration selectivity on the basis of quality. Section IV compares the different categories of respondents in terms of specified measures of aptitude and achievement. It is clear from these figures that in general there is no tendency for West Virginia's better qualified college graduates to leave the state. In fact, *virtually no difference can be observed between the qualifications of those leaving and those remaining in the state.*

The results thus indicate quite clearly that, among West Virginia college graduates in 1969, there was no systematic difference between average and exceptional individuals with respect to either subjective geographic preferences or the relative importance of nonpecuniary factors in different areas. It should be noted, however, that the nonpecuniary factors might become more important when individuals with large differences in training are considered (e.g., college graduates versus high school graduates). The present results, therefore, are not incompatible with the existence of a migration pattern which selects more heavily from college than high school graduates.

Motivation: Section V, which relates to the determinants of job location, is admittedly difficult to interpret. Theoretically, an individual will consider both economic and noneconomic factors when selecting his place of employment. Some individuals may place very little emphasis on one or the other of these factors but it is unlikely that a major portion of any group of college graduates will ignore either of them completely. What does it mean then to say that *either* economic *or* noneconomic factors were of primary importance in selecting a job location? The answer will ordinarily relate to the specific decision which was made (or anticipated) and thus does not preclude the possibility that the opposite answer would be given under different conditions. That is to say, individuals do not answer a question of this type by considering the weights they might apply to these two factors under all possible circumstances. Instead, they choose as most important the factor or factors which swung the balance in the case at hand.

It is not surprising to find that roughly 50 percent of the respondents in all categories judged economic and noneconomic considerations to be equally important. It is somewhat surprising to find that 26 percent of those already employed in West Virginia, and an identical percentage of those already employed out of state, had based their decisions primarily on economic grounds. The significant salary difference favoring out-of-state areas leads one to expect that a larger portion of those leaving would be motivated primarily by economic considerations. Apparently this is not the case.

In relation to the importance of economic considerations the figures show a significant difference between those who already have accepted jobs and those who have yet to search for or locate jobs. Economic considerations were more important to a significantly larger proportion of those who had already accepted employment. Since individuals attending graduate or professional schools represented a large portion of the persons who had not accepted employment, the results may indicate that these individuals place less emphasis on economic factors than do persons not planning to continue their education. It is also possible that salary offers vary more than is anticipated by potential job applicants.

A comparison between the noneconomic environment in West Virginia and that in other areas was responsible for a significant number of college graduates moving out of state. The factors under this heading, i.e., general living conditions, the availability of recreational and cultural facilities and the adequacy of government services, prompted 168 persons to move out of state whereas only 66 of those choosing to remain in the state regarded these factors as crucial elements in their decisions. Thus, on balance, the state's noneconomic environment was considered relatively inferior by these individuals. This conclusion should not be overemphasized since the great majority of the sample did not regard the noneconomic environment as the primary factor in their location decision.

The categories listed under "other" are of a much more specific nature. The location decision for 10 percent of the graduates was dictated by the job location of their husbands. Personal attachment and family businesses kept over 70 graduates within the state and accounted for the out-migration of less than 40 persons. If the proportions exhibited by the respondents hold for the entire group of graduates, personal factors will keep 213 persons in West Virginia and cause only 117 to leave. A significant number of individuals, approximately 3 percent on the average, cited the availability of employment in a specific occupation as the deciding factor. However, as the results in section VI indicate, this is a serious understatement for individuals locating outside the state.

Inducements to Return: In section VI, factors capable of inducing individuals to return to West Virginia are placed in five separate groups.[2] The first group is com-

---

[2] In relation to the inducements to return (question 6), there was virtually no difference between those who had accepted employment out of state and those who planned ultimately to do so. Accordingly, the responses for both groups were combined for purposes of analysis.

Although a number of multiple answers were received to question 6, only the first factor listed has been included in the Table 1 results. This causes an understatement to occur in some of the individual categories but the relative importance of the five major

posed of those who would not return under any conditions and those who would demand a salary premium before returning. This group, comprising 28 percent of the total, obviously has been unfavorably impressed by living conditions in West Virginia. Unless a marked change in attitude occurs, it is unlikely that many persons in this group will return to the state.

The second group, which accounts for 30 percent of the total, includes persons who migrated (or plan to migrate) primarily because of the lack of economic opportunities in the state. They do not demand an economic premium for returning but simply an approach to economic equality with other areas. In other words, this group seems to prefer the noneconomic aspects of life within West Virginia, and they would gladly return if what seemed to them to be the state's relative economic disadvantages were reduced to acceptable proportions.

The third group, representing 18 percent of the total, was dissatisfied with the general socio-economic-political environment of the state. The fact that individuals in this group would consider returning to West Virginia if certain improvements were made sets them apart from the first group. The changes specified, however, by some persons in the third group are so drastic that their accomplishment is highly unlikely.

The remaining 24 percent are divided equally among

groups would not be changed greatly by including second, third and fourth responses. It was quite common, for instance, for an individual to list all factors associated with the general socio-economic-political environment of the state.

those who might return for personal reasons and those who fall into more than one of the first three groups.

In summary, there exists a sizable group of migrants (30 to 40 percent) who are very unlikely to return to the state. At the same time, there is an equally sizable group with an active desire to return if certain changes are forthcoming. Improved economic opportunities alone would result in the re-migration to West Virginia of the majority of this group.

Separate Majors

Table 2 presents a breakdown according to the students' majors in college.[3] There are a number of similarities and differences among the four major fields of study. There was a heavy concentration of males in Commerce and Engineering, and of females in Education. The level of parental education was lowest in Engineering but did not differ appreciably among the other three majors. The proportion of West Virginia natives in the major ranged from 50 to 60 percent over the four groups. A majority of the individuals in each major field either had accepted a job or were in the process of entering the job market.[4]

[3] Figures are given only for those major fields containing at least 100 respondents. The fields omitted were Physical Education (97), Creative Arts (78), Agriculture and Forestry (40), and Journalism (33). Marked differences between these majors and the four covered in Table 2 will be presented in footnotes when there are enough observations to make the differences meaningful.

[4] Within the majors not presented in Table 2, there was a heavy concentration of males in Agriculture and Forestry (95%)

Differences in Ability: Aptitude and achievement scores again completely fail to support the contention that the best of West Virginia's college graduates are leaving the state. Only in the field of Commerce did the college grade point average of those who had accepted jobs outside the state exceed the average of those accepting jobs within the state. The precollege examination scores do not present as consistent a picture, but the instances in which out-of-state scores exceed their West Virginia counterparts, e.g., engineering CEEB quantitative scores, occurred very infrequently. The data relating to persons who had not yet accepted jobs also did not reveal any consistent superiority of those planning to leave the state over those planning to remain. The six differences between mean scores which were statistically significant at the 5 percent level were divided equally between those showing higher scores for persons locating in West Virginia and those showing higher scores for persons locating out of state. The results indicate very strongly that there is little, if any, difference between the ability of those who leave and the ability of those who remain.

Salary Differences: Mean salaries for the majors range from $9,235 in Engineering to $6,490 in Human Re-

and Journalism (64%). A majority (60%) of the Creative Arts majors were female. On the average, the level of parental education was similar to that of the majors listed. The proportion of students accepting jobs or entering the job market was significantly lower in Agriculture and Forestry (42%) and Journalism (47%). A larger portion (75%) of the Journalism majors were native West Virginians.

sources. Only in the major with the lowest mean salary, Human Resources, does the West Virginia mean exceed the out-of-state mean. The remaining three majors exhibit advantages to the out-of-state means ranging from $667 in Arts and Sciences to $812 in Commerce, with Engineering falling in between at $728.[5] There is no readily apparent explanation for this deviation on the part of the Human Resources major. Achievement test scores and college GPA's do show that, within this major, those planning to seek work out of state scored higher than those who already have accepted work out of state. This difference does not appear among those locating and planning to locate within West Virginia. But it is doubtful that the relationship between these measures of ability and salary is consistent enough to explain the higher in-state salaries in this major.[6]

Migration Rates: When migration rates are examined by major field of study, two definite patterns emerge. First, there is a marked difference among majors in the

[5] Among the majors not listed in Tables 2-5, one salary difference between West Virginia and out-of-state areas was significant at the 5 percent level. Creative Arts showed a $762 advantage for West Virginia.

[6] An examination of all questionnaires listing salaries of $10,000 and above produced a Human Resources major working as a split end for the Miami Dolphins at $17,500 and an Arts and Sciences major earning $25,000 operating his own business. Removing these two individuals from the sample would reduce the out-of-state means in Human Resources to $6,324 and Arts and Sciences to $7,157. This illustrates that the major categories are not perfectly homogeneous.

proportion of individuals remaining in West Virginia. Roughly 30 percent of the Commerce and Engineering graduates who had already accepted employment remained in the state, whereas over half of the Arts and Science and Education majors accepted jobs in West Virginia.[7] Similar but much smaller differences in out-migration rates were present among those who planned to seek jobs in the future. Second, in Arts and Sciences and Education the tendency to remain in West Virginia was far stronger among those who already had accepted employment than it was among those who planned to seek jobs in the future.

The basic difference in migration patterns between majors could be due to differences in the proportion of females in the various majors. Majors with high out-migration rates contain very few females relative to majors with low out-migration rates. The difference in migration patterns, therefore, could be the result of a consistently greater propensity to migrate on the part of males. In other words, if both males and females exhibit the same migration rates in all majors, and if the male rate is greater than the female rate, then majors with a high proportion of males would automatically exhibit relatively high out-migration rates. Furthermore, under these circumstances, the differences in migration rates among majors would be attributable solely to difference in the sex composition of the majors.

[7] The percentage of job holders locating in West Virginia from the four majors not covered in Table 2 ranged from 43 to 53 percent.

Data presented in Table 3 strongly indicates that the sex distribution among majors is not responsible for the observed differences in migration rates. For the total sample, female out-migration rates are all lower than their male counterparts, but the difference is quantitatively significant only among natives who already have accepted jobs. In addition, there is no consistent difference between male and female out-migration rates within the individual's major fields. In Commerce, with one exception,[8] the female rates are smaller than the male rates and the differences are quite large. But, in Education, the female rates are uniformly larger than the male rates. Arts and Sciences presents a mixed picture. The female rate is lower for those who have accepted jobs, but, on balance, there is very little difference among those who have yet to seek jobs.

Essentially, then, there is no general tendency for a higher proportion of females to remain in West Virginia. Furthermore, the tendency toward higher migration rates in Commerce and Engineering persists when males and females are observed separately. The only exception occurs among females seeking jobs, and there are very few Commerce observations involved in this case.

The figures in Table 4 demonstrate that the distribution of natives and nonresidents among majors is not responsible for the observed differences in out-migration rates. There is very little difference in the percent native

---

[8] The exception is the nonresident category for those who had accepted jobs. There were only four females in this category.

among majors in the accepted job category. Among those who will seek jobs, the percent native does not bear a consistent relationship to the migration rate. The observed migration patterns, therefore, must have emanated from differences among majors in characteristics other than sex and precollege residence.

In Arts and Sciences and Education there is no simple explanation for the difference in migration rates between those accepting jobs and those seeking jobs. Approximately 70 percent of the Arts majors who had accepted jobs were natives but only 55 percent of those planning to seek jobs from this major came from West Virginia. This undoubtedly explains a portion of the difference for the Arts major since natives in general have a much lower migration rate than nonresidents. In Education, however, the proportion of natives differs very little between job holders and job seekers. In addition, the individual native and nonresident migration rates are both significantly higher for job holders in these fields. Thus, the higher proportion of natives among job seekers cannot be primarily responsible for the higher migration rates in this group. The answer may lie in the differences in occupational distributions between categories, but the questionnaire results do not provide the information necessary to check upon this possibility.

Salary differences between West Virginia and out-of-state areas undoubtedly contributed to the outmigration of college graduates; however, they do not provide a complete explanation for the marked differences in migration rates among majors. This is illustrated by the fact that out-of-state salaries exceeded West Virginia salaries by almost as much in Arts and Sciences as they did in Commerce and Engineering. The high proportion of teachers in Education (90+ percent) and Arts and Sciences (40+ percent) may have contributed to the observed differences since job opportunities for teachers are relatively more plentiful in West Virginia. A description of the section V and VI results (not presented in Table 2) may aid further in identifying causal factors which may have been important in generating the observed migration patterns.

Motivation: Approximately 30 percent of the Commerce and Engineering majors listed economic considerations as the prime determinant of job location. Only 20 percent of the Human Resources majors,[9] and 15 percent of the Arts and Sciences majors cited this factor.[10] Thus higher out-of-state salaries seem to have been more important to Commerce and Engineering majors than to Arts and Sciences majors. In the case of Human Resources, the heavy concentration of women caused the location of their husbands' jobs to be much more important than it was in any of the other majors. Over 23

[9] Among the Human Resources majors, those staying in the state were much less concerned with economic factors than were those leaving the state.

[10] These figures are not indicative of the total importance of economic factors since a majority of all individuals in the sample judged economic and noneconomic considerations to be equally important.

percent of the Human Resources majors placed primary emphasis on this factor. The figures for the other majors were: Arts and Sciences, 10 percent; Commerce, 4 percent; and Engineering, less than one percent. This factor, however, does not explain the larger proportion of individuals remaining in West Virginia for either Human Resources or Arts and Sciences majors. In both of these majors, the spouse's job location was more important in moving individuals out of state than it was in keeping them in the state.[11] Personal ties (family businesses and personal attachment) were somewhat more important among Arts and Sciences (6 percent) and Human Resources (5.3 percent) majors than among Commerce (3.8 percent) and Engineering (2.9 percent) majors. But these percentages are too small to explain a major portion of the location differences among majors.

The importance of economic considerations is further illustrated by the list of factors capable of inducing individuals to return to West Virginia. There is a marked difference between majors in relation to the importance of the Group II factors (see Table 1) which represent

---

[11] If the husband's job location is as important to education majors in other states as it was to those in West Virginia, then the questionnaire results undoubtedly understate the impact of economic factors upon the teacher "shortage" in West Virginia. The general lack of economic opportunities in West Virginia will diminish the movement of college trained males from other areas into the state. The supply of teachers in West Virginia will be reduced each time a male with a teaching wife fails to locate in the state due to a lack of economic opportunities.

the lack of economic opportunities within West Virginia. Proportions of the majors citing this group of factors are as follows: Human Resources, 23 percent; Arts and Sciences, 27 percent; Commerce, 33 percent; and Engineering, 40 percent. Over 23 percent of the Engineering majors indicated they would return to West Virginia if a position utilizing their special training were made available to them.[12] The consistency of this picture is somewhat upset by the fact that higher salaries were listed as an inducement to return by 19 percent of the Human Resources majors whereas this factor was cited by only 10 to 12 percent of the other three majors.[13]

Natives and Nonresidents

Table 5 presents the results obtained when the questionnaire data were broken down according to high school location. Many of the differences between students attending high school in West Virginia (natives) and students attending high schools out of state (nonresidents) are quite predictable. Others seem to require some explanation. Only three of the characteristics

[12] This also seems to have been quite important to Agriculture and Forestry and Creative Arts majors.

[13] The only other marked difference among majors with respect to the Section VI, Table 1 inducements occurred in the "nothing" category. Approximately one-fifth of the Commerce and Arts and Sciences majors indicated that nothing could induce them to return to the state. Less than one-tenth of the Human Resources and Engineering majors gave this reply.

Survey Results

listed in the first three sections of Table 5 exhibit significant differences between natives and nonresidents: father's education, salary, and job location.

Fathers of nonresidents were more likely to have both attended and graduated from college than were the fathers of natives. This may simply reflect an economic bias in the selection of nonresident students. It is more expensive for nonresidents to attend college in West Virginia and the positive relationship between education and income is well known.

The average salary differences between natives and nonresidents are interesting. Natives locating in West Virginia earned $400 less per year than did nonresidents who located in the state. But natives locating out of state earned $400 more than nonresidents who also located out of state. The ability differences shown in Table 5 are not perfectly consistent with this salary pattern.[14] In addition, the significance of these ability differences is difficult to evaluate. The difficulty arises because of the marked difference in the proportions of natives and nonresidents taking the CEEB and ACT tests. Approximately 90 percent of the natives took the ACT test and 10 percent took the CEEB test. The corresponding percents for nonresidents were 25 and 75. Ability differences may have contributed to the observed salary pattern but it also appears that, *on the*

---

[14] Five of the eight ability comparisons are in the "right" direction but the remaining three show higher ability measures for the lower salary categories.

average, individuals do have a definite preference for locating in familiar territory.

The largest and most important difference relates to job location. Among those who already had jobs, 64 percent of the natives and only 21 percent of the nonresidents were locating in West Virginia. Since migration rates differ markedly among majors, it is possible that native-nonresident rate differences merely reflect the distribution of these groups among major fields. This possibility was investigated using the data presented in Table 6.

The Table 6 figures show that the nonresident out-migration rate exceeded the resident rate by a considerable amount in each of the eight major fields of study. Furthermore, a more refined method of examining these distributional differences indicates there was a very slight tendency for nonresident students to concentrate more heavily in the major fields characterized by relatively *low* out-migration rates.[15] Thus none of the overall native-nonresident difference in the out-migration rate results from nonresidents concentrating in fields characterized by high out-migration rates.

Once again, the measures of ability fail to exhibit a consistent difference between those locating in West Virginia and those leaving the state. The differences present are almost equally divided between those favoring the migrants and those showing higher ability among individuals remaining in the state.

[15] See Appendix B.

Survey Results

When natives and nonresidents are viewed separately, an interesting (if not perfectly consistent) tendency seems to emerge. The better qualified individuals are somewhat more likely to locate away from their original residence, i.e., the better qualified natives tend to locate out of state and the better qualified nonresidents in West Virginia. This tendency was quite pronounced among nonresidents who had already accepted employment. It was also present in the ACT scores for natives, a group encompassing the great majority of the native sample. This tendency however, was completely absent among the large group of nonresidents who had not yet accepted employment. Nevertheless, it appears that the absence of overall quality selectivity in migration is at least partially the result of these offsetting tendencies between natives and nonresidents. Our speculation relating to the causes of this pattern has produced nothing that is very convincing.

The results of sections V and VI (not presented in Tables 6 and 7) do not support many substantive observations. Personal attachment to the area caused more natives to locate in West Virginia and more nonresidents to locate out of state. Approximately 20 percent of the nonresidents who chose to remain in West Virginia did so because of their spouse's job location. This, however, is quantitatively unimportant since these individuals represent only 4 percent of the total number of nonresident students.

Under inducements to return there are three major differences which should be noted. Over 18 percent of the nonresidents, but only 8 percent of the natives, stated that nothing would induce them to return to West Virginia. Similarly, 11 percent of the natives, but less than 6 percent of the nonresidents, felt they might return because of family or personal ties. Neither of these differences is unexpected. Finally, 32 percent of the natives and 22 percent of the nonresidents indicated that improvements in the Group II factors (see Table 1) measuring economic opportunity within the state might induce them to return. All three differences simply seem to reflect the basic differences in locational preference between natives and nonresidents.

Attitudes Toward West Virginia

A letter accompanied the questionnaire inviting the respondents to comment on their attitudes toward West Virginia. Comments made by 323 respondents were so diverse that no attempt was made to categorize and tabulate them. Since the comments had no consistent structure it is conceivable that their interpretation may be affected by the biases of the investigator. Needless to say, an attempt was made to minimize this bias. In addition, since these respondents represent approximately 5 percent of the state's graduating seniors, it is quite possible their views are not typical, in all respects, of all those graduating from West Virginia colleges. Nevertheless, the group is sizable enough to warrant placing some emphasis on generalizations emanating from their comments.

The comments ranged from one brief sentence to

well-organized 300-word essays. There were very few vitriolic outbursts. The general impression was one of concerned students attempting to give honest and useful accounts of their feelings toward West Virginia.

The great majority of the commenting students expressed affection for and attachment to the state. This was true of native West Virginians, students from other states, students leaving the state, and students remaining. Although sympathetic, many were at the same time quite critical of the state, but these critical comments were often made reluctantly and even apologetically. A sizable group of the graduates made it quite clear their decision to leave the state was, in a sense, forced upon them by the state's shortcomings. They left little doubt that they would return if these shortcomings were removed.

The most frequent criticisms were directed at the educational system, the cultural facilities, and the apathetic, complacent attitude of the public. The educational system was criticized most frequently and by two separate groups: prospective teachers and prospective parents. The parents were obviously concerned with obtaining what they considered to be a good education for their children. Many expressed the opinion that the West Virginia educational system was not capable of providing this, thus forcing them to leave the state. Many native West Virginians held this opinion and based it on their own experiences in the public schools of the state. Prospective teachers felt that salaries were low and working conditions were poor within West Virginia. A considerable number, however, did feel that the recent $1,000 per year increase in teachers' salaries was a significant step in the right direction. Criticism also was directed toward certification requirements which were regarded as unduly strict and irrelevant.

The respondents often associated the complacent attitude of the public with the corrupt political environment. In the case of cultural and transportation facilities the complaints were quite simple: these were regarded as inadequate.

Questions relating to race were not included in the questionnaire. But a small number of Negro respondents expressed the opinion that opportunities for Negroes were better in areas other than West Virginia. These comments were not emotional and seemed to be based on actual knowledge of employment practices in other areas. It was impossible, however, to determine what proportion of the respondents were Negro, and what proportion of Negro respondents held this view.

When respondents were placed into groups of teachers and nonteachers there was a very marked difference in the reasons given for leaving the state. Many of the nonteachers left because they knew of *no* job opportunities in their fields of specialization within the state. Some of these individuals stated that campus job interviewing by state firms was infrequent and unenthusiastic. This complaint was almost nonexistent in the case of teachers, except for those in the fields of art and music. Teachers left the state because better jobs were available elsewhere, not because there was a complete lack of jobs in West Virginia. It is not surprising that demand for certain specialized occupations is limited or nonexistent within the confines of a single state. This is a natural result of differences in industrial structure which often are generated by efficiency considerations. Furthermore, educational institutions do not and should not restrict their offerings to meet only the occupational needs of their immediately surrounding areas.

It appears evident, then, from the general comments elicited by the questionnaires that a significant portion of the college graduates leaving the state are doing so reluctantly and would gladly stay if the state could offer educational, cultural, and political institutions comparable to those in other states. The comments of those remaining in West Virginia support a slight modification of this statement. Many chose to stay because they felt West Virginia was making progress toward comparability with other states. Thus, a serious effort directed at the state's problems may suffice to keep some of the graduates from migrating.

Perhaps the greatest danger in the observed outmigration lies in its selective nature. Those who are leaving are very concerned with the problems confronted by the state and its people, but they feel powerless to improve things and so they leave. On the other hand, those who remain seldom mentioned the problems facing the state. Instead, they often expressed satisfaction with the very institutions and attitudes criticized by those who were leaving. Furthermore, some members of this group had obviously accepted an almost religious obligation to defend the status quo against criticism from "outsiders".

Boulding aptly summarizes the effect of this type of selectivity as follows: "When the easiest solution to a problem is to leave it behind, the people who are left behind are not likely to be very good at solving it."[16] It should be noted, however, that the individuals remaining behind may prefer to live with the area's problems rather than to experience the changes which inevitably seem to accompany solutions to those problems. This fact renders difficult the achievement of "progress" and it also raises the very basic question of how much and what types of "progress" should actually be sought.

In relation to the need for change within the state, one respondent effectively summarized what well may be the feelings of many West Virginians:

> I have a great attachment to the state. . . . This will ever be my "home". . . . I don't want to stay, however. . . . I suppose that if the West Virginians could reach a cultural, economic, and educational level that would make the state a desirable permanent home the very elements of the people that I feel so strongly about (their simplicity . . . their "quaintness" and basic friendly honesty) would be despoiled . . . leave it (the state) as it is and it is

---

[16] K. E. Boulding, "The 'National' Importance of Human Capital," in Walter Adams, editor, *The Brain Drain* (Macmillan and Company, 1968), p. 114; and Don Patinkin, "A Nationalist Model," *idem*, p. 104.

"special" but not a desirable home—change it and it loses its "specialness".

The apparent paradox confronting this individual is shared by a significant portion of our national population. It is repeatedly and heatedly alleged that our single-minded quest for economic growth and development has generated undesirable side effects which more than outweigh the benefits associated with the growth process. It cannot be denied that sometimes, and perhaps often, growth generates adverse side effects. But it must surely be incorrect to conclude that a nation or a state either has to accept passively all of the consequences related to "the" growth process, or to do without growth completely.

The amount of growth (or progress) attained would be precisely the amount necessary to maximize community satisfaction if the following held true: 1) all of the effects of growth were known in advance, 2) growth could be achieved in any desired amount, and 3) the body politic was capable of making rational decisions. The difficulty is, of course, that these conditions are never completely fulfilled. They do, however, hold true to some degree. Thus, we may make an intelligent attempt to arrive at "the" proper amount of growth and development for our communities. Given the obvious and severe economic problems of a state such as West Virginia, it seems quite likely that some degree of growth and development would yield net positive benefits to its residents.

Summary

There are no absolute standards that may be used to classify a given volume of out-migration as too large, too small, or just right. The appropriate amount of out-migration will depend upon the amount of in-migration and the local supply and demand for labor. These conditions will vary considerably from place to place; thus, the appropriate amount of out-migration will vary also. There is, however, no compelling reason to regard the observed volume of out-migration from West Virginia as being alarmingly large. Fifty-eight percent of the sample chose to leave West Virginia but 38 percent were originally from out-of-state areas. Thus there was a gross loss (in-migration has not been considered) amounting to approximately one-third of the college graduates who were natives. Furthermore, this out-migration definitely was not selective of the best among West Virginia's college graduates.

The relatively low level of effective demand within West Virginia for the skills possessed by the graduating seniors was a major cause of the out-migration which did occur. This is illustrated by the fact that (with the exception of the Human Resources major) there was, on the average, an appreciable salary premium associated with the decision to locate out of state. In addition, a significant number of individuals cited a lack of job opportunities within their chosen occupation as their reason for leaving the state.

When attention turns toward the state's ability to attract college graduates from other areas, noneconomic as well as economic factors loom potentially important. Many individuals would return to the state only if better employment opportunities were present. But many others stipulated improvements in public services and cultural amenities as changes which would induce their return to West Virginia.

Chapter 3

The Role of Public Policy

General Policy Considerations

We will assume there is cause for public concern and action if the out-migration of educated individuals causes a deterioration in the status of the remaining residents of the state. This criterion admittedly adopts a provincial point of view: it completely ignores the benefits which the out-migration confers upon individuals leaving the state and upon the areas to which those individuals move. A thorough-going application of the hedonistic calculus would take these benefits into account, but an analysis which ignores them actually may come closer to the political realities of the situation.

In some instances out-migration definitely will inflict direct and immediate costs on the state's remaining residents. This would occur, for instance, if medical doctors would leave in such numbers that adequate provision could not be made for the health needs of the remaining residents.[1] The results of the survey do not relate di-

---

[1] The problem, in fact, may become manifest in a slightly different form. Instead of doctors leaving the state and thereby causing a deterioration in the state's medical services, we are more

rectly to the medical profession; thus no specific conclusions pertaining to this case can be reached. It is evident, however, that losses of this type, although quite spectacular in nature, are likely to be important only in a small number of specific occupations. In fact, examples outside the medical profession do not come easily to mind.

The marked differences in locational preference observed between natives and nonresidents suggest a possible strategy in cases where an economic shortage exists within a given occupation. While it would at first appear that training for this occupation within the state should concentrate on natives, this conclusion may be a bit oversimplified. For instance, it is possible, that within this occupation, natives trained out of state are just as likely to locate in West Virginia as are natives trained in West Virginia. If this is correct, then internal training programs that concentrate on natives will be effective only to the extent that they induce more natives, regardless of training location, to enter the occupation in question. Such an effect is likely to be rather small. A better strategy might be to stimulate interest in the occupation on the part of natives and to acquaint them

likely to find that an adequate number of doctors originally fail to locate within the state. In principle the results are the same, a level of medical services which is regarded as inadequate in terms of what might have been. The situation as it actually exists may receive less attention than it deserves since it is easier for individuals to forego benefits they have never enjoyed than to lose services to which they already have been accustomed.

with the advantages of locating in the state after their training is complete. However, if the shortage is to be alleviated it will quite likely require policies which are unashamedly designed to make the state a more attractive place for the occupation in question. Detailed studies of individual occupations are necessary before a choice can be made among the various possible strategies.[2]

The tendency for out-migration rates to be high among nonresidents also has some bearing on nonresident tuition charges in public institutions of higher learning. It is not difficult to justify setting nonresident tuition below marginal cost if benefits are generated when nonresidents choose to remain in the area after completing their education. In general, however, this study shows that too few nonresidents remain in the area to justify lower charges. In certain fields of study this conclusion may not be valid. For example, the proportion of nonresidents in Agriculture and Forestry remaining in the state (see Table 6) may be large enough to justify relatively low tuition in this area, assuming the state derives significant benefits when such individuals do locate in the state. There may be educational and social reasons for encouraging nonresident enrollment

---

[2] For a discussion of the problem relating to the medical profession see Frederick W. Schaupp, *A Study of the Factors Influencing Outmigration of M.D. Graduates of West Virginia University 1962-1966*, Bureau of Business Research, West Virginia University, Morgantown, 1969.

which may be quite sufficient to justify relatively low nonresident tuition charges.

A further concern over the brain drain seems to be with effects which are rather indirect in nature. The loss of skilled and educated individuals may reduce the incomes of those remaining in the state either by lowering their productivity (external economies or bottlenecks) or by reducing the rate of economic growth experienced by the state. But neither of these eventualities will come to pass unless out-migration creates shortages of specific types of labor. The questionnaire results point strongly to the fact that much of the out-migration from West Virginia results from low levels of effective demand and thus does not lead to a labor shortage. Furthermore, it seems quite likely that if the volume of out-migration were sharply reduced, a significant amount of underemployment would result.[3]

In relation to the economic development or redevelopment of an area, it has been argued that a pool of skilled and trained labor is necessary to support the industrial base needed for sustained growth. It cannot be denied that growth requires skilled and trained labor; but it is incorrect to move from this statement of fact to the assertion that a plentiful supply of skilled labor will ensure rapid economic growth. A supply of skilled labor

[3] The volume of unemployment would, of course, rise also, but for present purposes the point to be stressed is that many individuals would be working at jobs not requiring the full range of their abilities, e.g., engineers working as draftsmen or accountants working as clerks.

is necessary but not a sufficient condition for growth. Also, the practice of stockpiling skilled labor seems a rather dubious strategy to follow. The resultant under- or unemployment would certainly not provide investors with a favorable picture of an area's potential.

Nor is it clear, especially in the case of a state or region within the United States, that stockpiling skilled manpower is the only way in which a sufficient supply can be generated for purposes of economic growth. It has often been observed that the nonpecuniary factors tending to hold people in their home environments are quite strong.[4] This definitely seems to be the case for many West Virginia natives. Thus, although economic inducements causing many West Virginians to leave were quite strong, an improvement in economic opportunities within the state undoubtedly would cause some of these same persons to return. If the results of the current questionnaire are even roughly applicable to past time periods, there must exist a substantial pool of skilled and trained West Virginia natives who are employed outside the state and who would welcome the opportunity to return if the proper economic opportunity presented itself.

It is therefore unreasonable to argue that the lack of educated and trained manpower is a crucial element contributing to the economic problems of West Virginia. An adequate supply of labor could be easily attracted if

---

[4] See, for example, H. G. Johnson, "An Internationalist Model," in Walter Adams, editor, *The Brain Drain* (Macmillan and Company, 1968), pp. 70, 79.

the other factors necessary for sustained economic growth were present.[5] Moreover, an intemperate use of artificial methods designed to keep educated people in the state, aside from being unnecessary, is more likely to emphasize the basic weakness of the state's economic position than to generate the sought after improvements.[6]

Public Sector Employment

The complications arising from employment in the public sector of the economy require special consideration.[7] This is an area which could be treated naively by

[5] The identification of these "other factors" is beyond the scope of this paper, but it may be noted that the items listed under sections VI-VIII of Table 1, are undoubtedly of some importance, particularly because the educated individuals included in this survey consider them to be so.

[6] The discussion in the text has purposely ignored the fact that the individuals most concerned about the state's problems are leaving the state in large numbers. This has the dual effect of rendering progress more difficult to achieve and at the same time reducing the aspiration level of the remaining population. On the other hand it has been noted that the state is retaining many of the most capable of its college graduates. Thus, if the selectivity of migration is rendering difficult the achievement of progress, it is having this effect by removing the inclination to advance rather than the ability to do so. There are obvious difficulties involved in evaluating a lack of progress which is, at least in part, the result of a conscious choice made by individuals who do not desire progress.

[7] The British medical system affords perhaps the most striking example of the difficulties which may be generated by govern-

assuming that public officials intelligently set salaries to generate a desired volume and quality of public employment. If this were the case, then only temporary deviations from desired magnitudes would occur and these would present little cause for concern. It would be difficult, however, to take such an argument seriously, particularly in the case of the public school teachers in West Virginia.[8]

The out-migration of teachers is often regarded as a factor contributing to the teacher "shortage" in West Virginia. While this may be descriptively accurate, it represents a very superficial view of the problem. The root causes of the "shortage" must be sought in the motivation which prompts out-migration. Teachers are hesitant to locate in West Virginia because salaries are low and working conditions are poor in comparison with a number of nearby states. Low salaries alone will not result in a "shortage" of teachers in the conventional sense of the term. It is almost always possible to find someone to fill teaching positions, even where salaries are extremely

ment dictated wage rates. For a brief discussion of this case see H. G. Johnson, "The Economics of the 'Brain Drain': The Canadian Case," *Minerva*, Vol. 3, No. 3 (Spring 1965), pp. 302-3.

[8] The situation in the public schools of West Virginia may have changed significantly since the beginning of this study. Teachers' salaries in West Virginia are certainly more competitive today than they have been in the past. This is illustrated by the lack of a West Virginia out-of-state salary differential in the Human Resources and Education major. It is doubtful, however, that recent changes have rendered the text discussion completely inapplicable.

low. But it is not always possible to hire individuals who meet "minimum acceptable standards." It is this inconsistency between salary schedules and the qualifications regarded as acceptable for public school teachers which generates the teacher "shortage".

Out-migration is not the only problem involved in hiring qualified public school teachers. West Virginia, and other states as well, must compete with nonacademic employers for their teaching staffs. The unevenness of this competition is illustrated by the Table 7 data. Teachers' salaries generally are lower than nonteachers' salaries and the differential is much more pronounced among males. Among females the salary differences are quite small, particularly in view of the fact that teachers work from one to two months less per year than do nonteachers. This distinction by sex also is reflected in the ability measures. The better qualified males definitely gravitate away from the teaching profession. But the teacher-nonteacher ability differences are not as great for females and they are not consistently in one direction or the other.

It is quite clear that job opportunities outside the teaching profession are much more limited for females than they are for males. Furthermore, the use of a single salary schedule precludes the possibility of male-female wage differentials in teaching. It follows then that it would be much easier to hire qualified female teachers than to hire qualified male teachers. The ability figures from our limited sample provide weak support for this conclusion. Thus low teachers' salaries may not only cause a geographic out-migration of teachers but also a reduction in the overall number of qualified teachers and a female dominated teaching profession.[9]

In light of these considerations, it is quite reasonable to argue that the teacher "shortage" is not, in a real sense, a shortage at all. It is simply one of an almost infinite number of situations in which individuals would like to possess more of a commodity than they are willing to pay for. If there is a bona fide problem associated with public education in West Virginia, it stems from the public's unwillingness, or inability, to pay for the type of education desired.[10] The out-migration of teachers is a result of this unwillingness rather than a cause of the teacher "shortage". Salary increases and improved working conditions would seem to be the best means of ensuring an adequate supply of qualified teachers.[11]

---

[9] For a discussion of the feminizing influence of schools see Patricia Sexton, *Feminized Male: Classrooms, White Collars and The Decline of Manliness* (New York: Random House, 1969).

[10] In many of the poorest areas of the state, inability to finance public education is definitely the major problem.

[11] Given the fiscal problems confronting many areas within the state, it is surprising that variable salary schedules for different teaching fields have not been considered. The practice of applying a single salary schedule to all teachers makes the task of hiring "qualified" teachers far more expensive than it need be. Under a single salary schedule it is necessary to pay all teachers a salary which is high enough to attract qualified teachers in the specialized field which, in a sense, has the smallest supply of teachers available. This will obviously prove more costly than a variable

Summary

We have suggested that the legitimate areas for public concern over the "brain drain" in West Virginia are limited to specific occupations where it can be demonstrated that out-migration has, or will, inflict significant costs on the residents of the state. Although no attempt was made to identify these occupations, casual empiricism provided only the medical profession as an example.

In general, the out-migration of skilled and trained individuals seems to be based on economic factors and an artificial curtailment of this out-migration would undoubtedly introduce employment problems. Furthermore, there appears to be no advantage in artificially curtailing this migration.

In general, it appears that inaction is the appropriate course to follow. But to accept this suggestion one would be directly confronted with a public attitude which definitely regards the "brain drain" as a problem requiring immediate attention. It might be very difficult to gain public acceptance for a policy which explicitly proposed to do nothing about the "brain drain". But it should not prove impossible to at least avoid excessive

---

salary schedule tailored to the different supply conditions in the various specialized fields. The cost difference between the two types of salary schedules will, under most circumstances, be quite significant. For a detailed discussion of the economic aspects of variable salary schedules see Joseph Kershaw and Roland McKean, *Teacher Shortages and Salary Schedules* (McGraw-Hill, 1962).

criticism of a policy which simply does nothing without explicitly so stating. In fact, such a policy would represent little change from the existing situation in terms of effectiveness. Needless to say, the publicity currently emanating from official sources which stresses the questionable negative effects of the brain drain should be replaced either with silence or with statements emphasizing the positive aspects of out-migration.

Tables

1—Total Sample

2—Questionnaire Results by Major Field of Study

3—Male, Female and Total Migration Rates by Major, High School Location and Job Status

4—Distribution of Individuals by Sex, Major, High School Location and Job Status

5—Questionnaire Results for Natives and Nonresidents

6—Native and Nonresident Migration Rates and Distributions by Major Field of Study

7—Ability and Salary Measures for Teachers and Nonteachers by Sex and Major Field

TABLE 1

TOTAL SAMPLE

I. Number of respondents, *2,215*; Male, *1,148 (52.0%)*; Female, *1,057 (48.0%)*.

II.
A. Number attending high school in West Virginia, *1,243 (62.0%)* of all respondents.
B. Number with one parent born in West Virginia, *1,264 (57.5%)* of all respondents.
C. Number whose father i) went to college, *779 (35.4%)* of all respondents.
   ii) graduated from colleges, *517 (23.5%)* of all respondents.

III. Number of individuals who planned to:
A. Enter military service, *162 (7.5%)* of all respondents.
B. Attend Graduate School, *435 (20.1%)* of all respondents.
   i) in West Virginia, *140*; ii) out of state, *195*; percent of graduate students in West Virginia, *41.8*.
C. Enter the job market, *668 (30.9%)* of all respondents.
   i) in West Virginia, *243*; ii) out of state, *380*; percent of job seekers in West Virginia, *39.0*
D. A, B, and C will eventually enter the job market.
   i) in West Virginia, *467*; ii) out of state, *752*; percent planning to seek jobs in West Virginia, *38.3*.
E. Go to a job already accepted, *891 (41.2%)* of all respondents.
   i) in West Virginia, *415*; ii) out of state, *453*; percent of job holders in West Virginia, *47.8*
   Average salary 1) in West Virginia, *$6,857**; 2) out of state, *$7,707**.

IV.

Average Values For:	1 Total	2 Graduate School	3 Military Service	4 Entering Job Market	5 Accepted Job in W.Va.	5 Accepted Job Out of State	6 2,3,4 Will Seek Job in W.Va.	6 2,3,4 Will Seek Job Out of State
Composite ACT Score	23.09	24.88	23.10	22.51	22.11	22.70	22.34*	23.96*
CEEB Verbal Score	512.48	539.61	524.40	504.52	527.72*	490.29*	530.31	517.72
CEEB Quantitative Score	548.83	557.34	568.50	529.77	574.43	557.67	544.31	544.90
College GPA Score	2.75	2.93	2.53	2.71	2.78	2.70	2.75	2.74

* mean difference significant at the 5 percent level.

Table 1—Continued

		Accepted Job			Will Seek Job			
	in W.Va.		Out of State		in W.Va.		Out of State	
V. Determinants of Job Location	No.	%	No.	%	No.	%	No.	%
i. Economic considerations	106	25.9	118	26.0	75	16.1	87	11.6
ii. Noneconomic considerations	16	3.9	43	9.5	50	10.7	125	16.6
iii. i) and ii) equally important	196	47.9	227	50.0	224	48.0	402	53.5
iv. Other								
1. Husbands (or Wives) job (or school) location	41	10.0	39	8.6	53	11.3	75	10.0
2. Family business	9	2.2	2	.4	8	1.7	16	2.1
3. Job availability in selected occupation	14	3.4	10	2.2	12	2.6	25	3.3
4. Personal attachment stemming from previous residence in area	20	4.9	8	1.8	34	7.3	13	1.7
5. Miscellaneous	7	1.7	7	1.6	11	2.4	9	1.2
Total	409	99.9	454	100.1	467	100.1	752	100.2

VI. Factors Which Would Induce Individuals to Return to West Virginia

			No.	%
i 28%	1	Nothing	184	16.07
	2	A higher salary	137	11.97
ii 30%	3	Availability of a position in which specified training would be utilized	128	11.18
	4	Better job opportunities	114	9.96
	5	A comparable salary	57	4.98
	6	Better opportunities as defined under i in Question 5	47	4.10
iii 18%	7	Better public schools	68	5.94
	8	Improvements in state and local governments	42	3.67
	9	Better roads	37	3.23
	10	Better cultural and recreational facilities	33	2.88
	11	Better opportunities as defined under ii in Question 5	21	1.83
iv 12%	12	Husband's job location	73	6.38
	13	Family or personal ties	61	5.33
v 12%	14	Better opportunities as defined under i and ii in Question 5	50	4.37
	15	Improvement in the standard of living	41	3.58
	16+	Miscellaneous	52	4.54
		Total	1145	100.01

+ With the exception of factor number 11, all responses accounting for less than 2 percent of the total were grouped under Miscellaneous. They were 1) change in attitude of people, 2) establishment of a more active business climate, 3) better opportunities to pursue an advanced degree and 4) relaxation of teacher certification requirements.

TABLE 2
QUESTIONNAIRE RESULTS BY MAJOR FIELD OF STUDY

	Arts and Sciences	Human Resources and Education	Commerce	Engineering and Mines
Number of respondents Male Female	994 (45.1%)+ 489 (49.2%) 505 (50.8%)	430 (19.5%)+ 59 (13.7%) 369 (86.3%)	389 (17.6%)+ 318 (81.7%) 71 (18.3%)	146 (6.6%)+ 141 (96.6%) 5 (3.4%)
Number attending High School in West Virginia	550 (55.2%)	261 (60.7%)	203 (52.1%)	89 (61.0%)
Number with one parent born in West Virginia	551 (55.4%)	256 (59.5%)	222 (56.9%)	97 (66.4%)
Number whose father: went to college graduated from college	358 (36.0%) 240 (24.1%)	122 (28.4%) 108 (25.1%)	133 (34.2%) 88 (22.6%)	35 (24.0%) 21 (14.4%)
Number who plan to: A. Enter Military Service	72 (7.2%)	9 (2.1%)	59 (15.2%)	4 (2.7%)
B. Attend graduate school	264 (26.6%)	41 (9.5%)	37 (9.5%)	27 (18.5%)
C. Enter job market	297 (29.9%)	166 (38.6%)	110 (28.3%)	8 (5.5%)

A, B, and C will enter job market:				
in West Virginia	216	76	64	9
out of state	299	126	121	21
percent to seek jobs in West Virginia	41.9%	37.6%	34.6%	30.0%
Go to accepted job				
in West Virginia	315 (31.7%)	209 (48.6%)	177 (45.5%)	106 (72.6%)
out of state	181	110	52	30
	126	96	125	71
percent job holders in West Virginia	59.0%	53.4%	29.4%	29.7%
Average salary				
in West Virginia	$6,654*	$6,534*	$7,534*	$8,707*
out of state	$7,321*	$6,443*	$8,346*	$9,435*

Table 2—Continued

College	Average Values for	Total	Accepted Job in W.Va.	Accepted Job out of State	Seek Job in W.Va.	Seek Job out of State
Arts and Science	Composite ACT score	24.01	22.96*	24.39*	23.00*	24.76*
	CEEB Verbal score	532.36	534.80	504.13	526.64	544.21
	CEEB Quant. score	552.22	561.44	561.80	547.88	549.54
	College GPA	2.84	2.85	2.78	2.84	2.81
Human Resources and Education	Composite ACT score	21.41	20.84	20.71	20.92	22.59
	CEEB Verbal score	498.71	564.00	488.48	536.60	499.97
	CEEB Quant. score	512.61	601.75*	502.41*	539.20	522.59
	College GPA	2.74	2.79*	2.62*	2.74	2.76
Commerce	Composite ACT score	23.00	22.04	21.45	22.60	24.04
	CEEB Verbal score	484.10	488.00	471.30	525.00	484.14
	CEEB Quant. score	563.31	647.83*	561.56*	540.00	561.35
	College GPA	2.60	2.59	2.69	2.56	2.52

Engineering and Mines	Composite ACT score	24.31	23.81	24.89	20.50	24.29
	CEEB Verbal score	491.27	448.33	497.38	.....	496.00
	CEEB Quant. score	611.68	509.50*	657.75*	.....	552.50
	College GPA	2.66	2.73	2.62	2.80	2.71

* Mean difference significant at the 5 percent level.
+ These percents relate to the total sample.
The numbers in parentheses represent the percent of the total number of individuals in the major.

TABLE 3

MALE, FEMALE AND TOTAL MIGRATION RATES BY MAJOR, HIGH SCHOOL LOCATION AND JOB STATUS

		Accepted Job			Will Seek Job		
		Native[1]	Non-Resident[2]	Total	Native[1]	Non-Resident[2]	Total
Arts and Science	Male	.286	.765	.449	.375	.845	.586
	Female	.195	.731	.385	.415	.838	.588
	Total	.232	.744	.412	.395	.841	.587
Human Resources and Education	Male	.125	.769	.342	.417	.857	.550
	Female	.330	.806	.506	.486	.902	.626
	Total	.290	.800	.476	.479	.897	.618
Commerce	Male	.643	.792	.714	.603	.909	.729
	Female	.400	1.000	.600	.378	.727	.471
	Total	.617	.807	.705	.516	.879	.658
Engineering	Male	.589	.931	.701	.632	.857	.700
	Female	*	*	*	*	*	*
	Total	*	*	*	*	*	*
Total	Male	.446	.799	.582	.460	.856	.626
	Female	.278	.779	.456	.443	.854	.603
	Total	.365	.789	.524	.451	.855	.614

[1] Native—high school in West Virginia.
[2] Non-Resident—high school out of state.
* Only males are reported upon since they represent 97 percent of the engineering sample.

TABLE 4

DISTRIBUTION OF INDIVIDUALS BY SEX, MAJOR, HIGH SCHOOL LOCATION AND JOB STATUS

		Natives[1]	Accepted Job Non-Resident[2]	Percent Native[1]	Native[1]	Will Seek Job Non-Resident[2]	Percent Native[1]
Arts and Sciences	Male	77	34	69.4	128	103	55.4
	Female	113	52	68.5	130	111	53.9
	Total	190	86	68.8	258	214	54.7
Human Resources and Education	Male	24	13	64.9	12	7	63.2
	Female	100	62	61.7	109	61	64.1
	Total	124	75	62.3	121	68	64.0
Commerce	Male	84	53	61.3	58	55	51.3
	Female	10	4	71.4	37	11	77.1
	Total	94	57	62.2	95	66	59.0
Engineering	Male	56	29	65.9	19	7	73.1
	Female	*	*	*	*	*	*
	Total	*	*	*	*	*	*
Total	Male	267	144	65.0	261	194	57.4
	Female	245	131	65.2	307	212	59.2
	Total	512	275	65.1	568	406	58.3

[1] Native—high school in West Virginia.
[2] Non-Resident—high school out of state.
* Only males are reported upon since they represent 97 percent of the engineering sample.

TABLE 5

QUESTIONNAIRE RESULTS FOR NATIVES AND NONRESIDENTS

	Natives	Non-Residents
Number of respondents	1,241 (56%)+	761 (34%)+
Male	611	394
Female	626	364
Number with one parent born in West Virginia	1,056 (85%)	98 (13%)
Number whose father:		
went to college	405 (33%)	310 (41%)
graduated from college	250 (20%)	219 (29%)
Number who plan to		
A. Enter the military service	79 (6%)	65 (9%)
B. Attend graduate school	241 (20%)	152 (20%)
C. Enter job market	369 (30%)	241 (32%)
A, B, and C will enter job market:		
in West Virginia	349	68
out of state	310	374
percent to seek jobs in West Virginia	53%	15%
Go to accepted job		
in West Virginia	522 (43%)	278 (37%)
out of state	327	58
percent to seek jobs in West Virginia	187	220
	64%	21%
Average salary		
in West Virginia	$6,796	$7,193
out of state	$7,910	$7,504

Table 5—Continued

Pre-College Residence	Average Values for	Total	Accepted Job in W.Va.	Accepted Job out of State	Seek Job in W.Va.	Seek Job out of State
Natives	Composite ACT score	22.95	21.97*	23.09*	22.35*	23.80*
	CEEB Verbal score	533.09	509.46	468.33	567.14	541.48
	CEEB Quant. score	554.63	529.92	519.09	573.67	584.54
	College GPA	2.79	2.79	2.73	2.77	2.79
Out of State	Composite ACT score	23.43	25.56*	21.56*	23.64	24.26
	CEEB Verbal score	510.73	534.04*	496.84*	504.70	515.91
	CEEB Quant. score	549.41	601.37	556.49	532.75	542.15
	College GPA	2.69	2.78*	2.65*	2.71	2.71

* Mean difference significant at the 5 percent level.
+ These percents relate to the total sample.
The numbers in parentheses represent the percent of the total number of individuals for the residence category.

TABLE 6
NATIVE AND NON-RESIDENT MIGRATION RATES AND DISTRIBUTIONS BY MAJOR FIELD OF STUDY

Major Field	1 Migration Rate Native	2 Migration Rate Non-Resident	3 Migration Rate Total	4 Number of Natives	5 Percent Distribution Native	6 Number of Non-Residents	7 Percent Distribution Non-Resident
Commerce	.56	.84	.67	197	16.8	128	17.8
Engineering	.55	.92	.67	85	7.2	38	5.3
Physical Education	.39	.82	.57	46	3.9	34	4.7
Human Resources	.37	.84	.54	253	21.6	144	20.0
Creative Arts	.37	.76	.54	40	3.4	29	4.0
Journalism	.46	.83	.53	24	2.0	6	.8
Arts Sciences	.34	.78	.51	509	43.4	323	44.9
Agriculture Forestry	.42	.53	.47	19	1.6	17	2.4
TOTAL	.40	.81	.56	1,173	99.9	719	99.9

TABLE 7

ABILITY AND SALARY MEASURES FOR TEACHERS AND NON-TEACHERS BY SEX AND MAJOR FIELD

All Majors

	Male Teachers	Male Non-Teachers	Female Teachers	Female Non-Teachers
ACT	20.82	23.49	21.80	22.53
CEEB Verbal	497	496	485	519
CEEB Quant.	528	597	511	536
GPA	2.72	2.68	2.79	2.81
Salary	$6,630	$8,358	$6,428	$6,701

Arts and Sciences

	Male Teachers	Male Non-Teachers	Female Teachers	Female Non-Teachers
ACT	22.65	24.96	23.10	22.71
CEEB Verbal	555	524	509	507
CEEB Quant.	486	602	538	545
GPA	2.69	2.77	2.97	2.85
Salary	$6,596	$7,823	$6,327	$6,795

Human Resources and Education

	Female Teachers	Female Non-Teachers
ACT	21.57	20.80
CEEB Verbal	474	548
CEEB Quant.	502	512
GPA	2.71	2.70
Salary	$6,509	$6,115

Table 7—*Continued*

Commerce

	Male	
	Teachers	Non-Teachers
ACT	18.00	21.81
CEEB Verbal	Na	479
CEEB Quant.	Na	580
GPA	2.57	2.65
Salary	$5,552	$8,150

All figures refer only to individuals reporting salaries.
Na—Not available.

Exhibit 1   *Appendix A*

April 1969

To All Graduating Seniors:

The enclosed questionnaire is part of a study relating to the migration of college graduates trained within the state of West Virginia. The Regional Research Institute of West Virginia University is supporting the project. Our primary concern is with the factors which influence an individual when he decides where he will live and work.

Your answers will be kept completely confidential. To ensure this, please *print* your name on the upper left-hand corner of the return envelope. When the envelope is received your name will be checked off a master list and the envelope will be immediately destroyed.

Finally, we will welcome any comments reflecting your attitudes toward West Virginia on the back of the questionnaire. Try to relate your comments to your decision to live and work either in or outside of West Virginia.

Your cooperation will be greatly appreciated.

                         Sincerely yours,
                         Richard Raymond
                         Director of Graduate
                         Programs in Economics

RR:bb
Enclosure

Exhibit 2

SENIOR JOB MIGRATION SURVEY

Division..Major..Sex:......M......F

Teaching Field (For education majors only)..

High School Location (county and state)..

Were either of your parents born in West Virginia? ....Yes ....No

Give a close approximation of the following if applicable:

    a) American College Testing Program Test Score (Composite ACT)..........

    b) College Entrance Examination Board Test Scores: Verbal..........

       Quantitative..........

    c) Cumulative college grade point average..........

Father's chief occupation while you lived at home..

Did your father attend college? ......Yes ......No   Did he graduate? A ......Yes ......No

1. Following graduation will you: (a) attend graduate or professional school, (b) go to a job already accepted, (c) enter the job market, or (d) enter military service. (Please circle appropriate letter.)

2. If (a), please indicate: Name of school..

3. If (b), please indicate: Name of employer..
   Location of your job (county or city, and state)..................................
   Position..Starting salary..........................

4. If (a), (c), or (d), in what state, or states, do you plan ultimately to concentrate your job search?..

5. In accepting your job, or in deciding where you will concentrate your job search, which of the following was or is *primarily* responsible for your decision? (Circle appropriate number.)
   (i) economic considerations—income, working conditions, opportunities for advancement, job security and other monetary considerations.
   (ii) non-economic considerations—general living conditions, the availability of recreational and cultural facilities (e.g., museums, concerts, the theater, etc.) and the adequacy of government services (e.g., public schools).
   (iii) economic and non-economic considerations were equally important.
   (iv) other (specify)..

6. If you are to be employed or seek employment outside West Virginia, what would induce you to return to West Virginia to live and work?..

Exhibit 3

College	Number Mailed	Number of Respondents	Percent
I. State			
1. Bluefield State College	136	34	25
2. Concord College	200	67	33.5
3. Fairmont State College	310	98	31.6
4. Glenville State College	223	66	29.6
5. Marshall University	812	255	31.4
6. Shepherd College	274	94	34.3
7. West Liberty State College	506	156	30.8
8. West Virginia Institute of Technology	327	119	36.4
9. West Virginia State College	238	68	28.6
10. West Virginia University	1,595	669	41.9
Total	4,621	1,626	35.2
II. Private			
1. Alderson-Broaddus College	102	55	53.9
2. Bethany College	232	87	37.5
3. Davis and Elkins College	146	52	35.6
4. Morris Harvey College	314	98	31.2
5. Salem College	244	65	26.6
6. West Virginia Wesleyan College	385	130	33.8
7. Wheeling College	200	45	22.5
Total	1,624	532	32.8
Grand Total	6,245	2,158	34.6

Appendix B

The procedure outlined in this appendix is designed to separate the effects of two distinct factors on the difference in out-migration rates between natives and nonresidents. These out-migration rates will differ because (1) natives and nonresidents will be concentrated in different major fields of study and (2) natives and nonresidents will have different propensities to leave the state in each major field of study. The quantitative significances of each factor may be isolated as follows: let

M_{Ni} = the out-migration rate of natives in major i

N_{Ni} = the number of natives in major i

M_{Fi} = the out-migration rate of nonresidents in major i

N_{Fi} = the number of nonresidents in major i

D = the difference between the overall nonresident and native out-migration rates

Z = the number of different major fields

The two overall out-migration rates are therefore

$$\text{Native} = \sum_{i=1}^{Z} M_{Ni} \cdot N_{Ni} \div \sum_{i=1}^{Z} N_{Ni}$$

76 *The Myth of the Appalachian Brain Drain*

$$\text{Nonresident} = \sum_{i=1}^{Z} M_{Fi} \cdot N_{Fi} \div \sum_{i=1}^{Z} N_{Fi}$$

and the difference, D, is

$$D = \frac{\sum_{i=1}^{Z} M_{Fi} \cdot N_{Fi}}{\sum_{i=1}^{Z} N_{Fi}} - \frac{\sum_{i=1}^{Z} M_{Ni} \cdot N_{Ni}}{\sum_{i=1}^{Z} N_{Ni}}$$

Now let K_i equal the difference between the nonresident and native out-migration rates in major field i or $K_i = M_{Fi} - M_{Ni}$; $M_{Fi} = M_{Ni} + K_i$

1) The nonresident out-migration rate may now be written

$$\text{Nonresident} = \frac{\sum_{i=1}^{Z} (M_{Ni} + K_i) \cdot N_{Fi}}{\sum_{i=1}^{Z} N_{Fi}}$$

$$\text{Nonresident} = \frac{\sum_{i=1}^{Z} M_{Ni} \cdot N_{Fi} + \sum_{i=1}^{Z} K_i \cdot N_{Fi}}{\sum_{i=1}^{Z} N_{Fi}}$$

Appendix B

$$\text{Nonresident} = \frac{\sum_{i=1}^{Z} M_{Ni} N_{Fi}}{\sum_{i=1}^{Z} N_{Fi}} + \frac{\sum_{i=1}^{Z} K_i N_{Fi}}{\sum_{i=1}^{Z} N_{Fi}}$$

and the difference becomes

$$D = \frac{\sum_{i=1}^{Z} K_i N_{Fi}}{\sum_{i=1}^{Z} N_{Fi}} + \left[\frac{\sum_{i=1}^{Z} M_{Ni} N_{Fi}}{\sum_{i=1}^{Z} N_{Fi}} - \frac{\sum_{i=1}^{Z} M_{Ni} N_{Ni}}{\sum_{i=1}^{Z} N_{Ni}} \right]$$

The first term represents the portion of D generated by differences in the nonresident and native out-migration rates within individual major fields.

The bracketed term represents the portion of D generated by the different distribution of the nonresident and native populations among major fields (the first term in brackets is simply the overall nonresident out-migration rate which would prevail if the nonresident and native rates were equal for each individual major field).

For the present, sample D is equal to .402. The first term has a value of .404 which indicates that the entire difference in out-migration rates results from higher nonresident rates in the individual major fields. The second term equals −.002 which for all practical purposes means that there was no difference in the distribution of natives and nonresidents among major fields.

The method presented above is conceptually equivalent to one which proceeds by expressing the native out-migration rate as a function of M_{Fi}, K_i and N_{Ni}. Using this alternative procedure, the value of the first term is .407 and the value of the second term is −.005. In this case, the procedures are, in essence, statistically as well as conceptually equivalent.